The wishing Adventure at sea

Written by William Edmonds
Illustrated by
Shelagh McNicholas and Robert McPhillips

Heinemann

Setting sail

It was a hot summer's day.
Yasmin, Jack and Lee were at the
swimming pool.
'I wish we were at the seaside,' said
Yasmin.
'I wish we could sail out to sea,' said Jack.
'I wish this rubber ring was a sailing ship,'
said Lee.

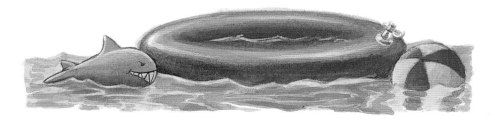

'Let's make a wish on the magic stone,'
said Yasmin, and she held out in her
hand a little stone. It was pink and
grey and blue, and in the middle was
a hole. Lee put his finger in the hole.
Then they all shut their eyes and
whispered, 'One ... two ... three ...
wish-sh-sh-sh.'

When Yasmin, Jack and Lee opened
their eyes they were on a ship sailing
out to sea. The ship had a big white
sail and at the top of the mast was
a little red flag.
'I wonder where we are going,'
said Yasmin.
'Let's follow those dolphins,' said Lee.

But then the wind began to blow a little harder and the waves grew bigger.

Up and down went the ship, up and down, up and down.

'I don't feel very well,' said Lee.

The wind blew harder and harder.
The waves grew even bigger and threw
the ship from side to side. The dolphins
swam off.

'Help!' shouted the children, as they
held on to the side of the ship.

'Help! Help!' they called out again,
and then there was a big CRASH!

The ship had hit some rocks by an
island and they had made a big hole in
the side of the ship.

'What can we do?' asked Yasmin.

'Let's go on to the island,' said Jack.

'We might find someone who can help us.'

Yasmin, Jack and Lee climbed off
the rocks and on to the sand. They saw
some tall trees.

'Coconuts!' shouted Jack, and he ran
over to the trees and found a coconut
on the sand.

After they had eaten the coconut,
Yasmin, Jack and Lee set off to look
around the island, but they didn't see
anyone. They sat down and Lee began
to dig in the sand.
'Look!' said Lee. 'I've found something.'
'It looks like gold,' said Jack.

Then all the children started to dig in the sand. Soon they found lots and lots of gold coins. Yasmin put the coins in a bag.

'We could take the bag home,' said Lee.

'But how are we going to get home?' asked Yasmin.

'I'll climb a tree and look out for a ship,' said Jack.

So Jack climbed up a tree and looked
out to sea. He could see a big ship.
He waved and waved and soon the ship
sailed over to the island.

'We lost our ship in a storm. Please
can you take us home?' asked Yasmin.
'Yes, come with me,' said the sailor.
So the children picked up the bag of
gold and climbed on to the ship.

Rescued!

The ship sailed out to sea. It had big
white sails and at the top of the mast
was a black and white flag.
'Look,' said Lee, 'I can see those
dolphins again.'

When they were right out at sea, the
sailor said, 'Ha! Ha! Ha! I am a pirate.
Now let's see what you've got in
that bag.'
He cut open the bag and out fell all the
gold coins.
'Gold!' shouted the pirate. 'That's just
what I want.'

'Now it's goodbye to you,' said the pirate, and he made Yasmin, Jack and Lee walk the plank. One by one they fell into the sea.

'Help!' they all shouted. 'Help! Help!'
But the pirate sailed away and didn't
even look back.

'What can we do now?' said Yasmin.

'Look,' said Lee, 'here come the three
dolphins.'

The dolphins swam up to the children.

'Climb on our backs,' said the dolphins,
'and we will take you to safe land.'

So Yasmin, Jack and Lee climbed on
the dolphins' backs and off they swam.

The dolphins swam very fast.
The children laughed and shouted as
the dolphins jumped in and out of
the water.

Suddenly Jack shouted, 'There's
something coming after us.'
'Oh no,' said Yasmin, 'it's a shark.'
The shark was getting nearer and nearer.
The dolphins swam as fast as they could,
and started jumping higher and higher
over the waves. Then with one last jump
they threw the children up into the sky.

BUMP!

The children landed on a little round island.

'At last we are safe,' said Lee. 'No more pirates. No more sharks.'

'Wait,' said Jack, 'this island is moving.'
'It's not an island at all,' said Yasmin.
'We're on the back of a giant whale.'
'HELP!' they all shouted.
Then, SPLASH! they all fell back into
the sea.

'What have you been doing?' asked Dad, as he came to the side of the pool and saw the children jumping off the ring and making a SPLASH! 'What was all that noise?'

'Well,' said Yasmin, 'it's a very long story.'